Choose the

Farthest Star

Choose the

Farthest Star

WORDS OF WISDOM FOR SUCCESS
BEYOND YOUR DREAMS

Bret Nicholaus and Paul Lowrie

Authors of the national bestseller *The Conversation Piece*

Warm Words Press

a division of William Randall Publishing

Warm Words Press
a division of William Randall Publishing
P.O. Box 340, Yankton, SD 57078

Cover, graphic, and text design by Ann Lundstrom
(www.demo-graphics-design.com)

ATTENTION: SCHOOLS AND BUSINESSES
William Randall books are available at quantity discounts with bulk
purchase for educational, business, or promotional use.
For more information, contact:
William Randall Publishing, Special Sales Department,
P.O. Box 340, Yankton, South Dakota 57078.

ISBN #0-9755801-2-4

Printed in the United States of America

First Edition: July 2004

10 9 8 7 6 5 4 3 2 1

Choose the Farthest Star

Introduction

Abraham Lincoln. Martha Washington. Thomas Edison. Helen Keller. Michelangelo. Mother Teresa. Leo Tolstoy.... Within the pages of the book you are currently holding, we have gathered together the wise words of many famous individuals (as well as some lesser known people) from different walks of life throughout the ages. Specifically, we have collected a sampling of those sayings that cover the spectrum of how we might define the word "success" and what steps a person could take that would move them in the direction of greater success in all areas of life.

We will be completely honest and say this at the outset: If you are looking for a book that describes success mainly in terms of how much money one can make, you've probably come to the wrong book. As you will see from the quotes contained in this collection, we believe that success means far more than—and, quite frankly, may be exclusive of—monetary gain. Success can be defined and achieved in such diverse ways as persisting in the face of difficulty, remaining happy even when circumstances are not what you'd like, having good character, helping others, not worrying about things beyond your control, etc.

While we, as the authors, believe that all these quotations have something to say that can lead you toward a more successful life, you will likely find that certain quotes speak more personally and powerfully to you than other quotes do. This is to be expected. Do realize, however, that a quotation that initially lacks deep meaning to you may become increasingly significant if you allow yourself to ponder the words a bit.

In the end, success certainly means different things to different people; it can even mean different things at different times in our own lives. It is our hope that, as you peruse the pages of this book, the words of these men and women will help you better define success, or perhaps completely re-define it. You might ultimately determine that success can be summed up in one simple sentence, or you may decide that true success is like a puzzle with numerous pieces that must all come together. Whatever you decide that success means for you, we hope that this book will inspire you to do all you can to achieve it in the days and years ahead.

Wishing you much success both now and always,

Bret Nicholaus and Paul Lowrie

It is not living that is important, but living rightly.

SOCRATES

The greater part of our happiness depends on our dispositions, and not our circumstances.

MARTHA WASHINGTON

Everyone is enthuastic at **times**. One person has enthusiasm for thirty **minutes**, another has it for thirty **days**. But it is the one who has it for thirty **years** who makes a success in life.

EDWARD BUTLER

When you reach
for the stars, you may
not quite get one;
but you won't come
up with a handful
of mud either.

LEO BURNETT

3

Even if you're on the right track, you'll get run over if you just sit there.

WILL ROGERS

Endeavor to live so that when you die, even the undertaker will be sorry.

MARK TWAIN

4

Trust in the Lord with all your heart, and **lean** not on your own understanding; in all your ways **acknowledge** Him, and He will **direct** your paths.

THE BIBLE, PROVERBS 3:5

Use the past as a guidepost, not a hitching post.

L. THOMAS HOLDCROFT

Everybody thinks of changing humanity, but nobody thinks of changing himself.

LEO TOLSTOY

Success comes before work only in the dictionary.

SOURCE UNKNOWN

Enjoy the little things, for one day you may look back and realize they were the big things.

ROBERT BRAULT

Each person is capable of doing one thing well. If he attempts several, he will fail to achieve distinction in any.

The most important thing I know is to surround myself with people who are smarter than I am.

CHARLES WALGREEN

Worry often gives a small thing a big shadow.

SWEDISH PROVERB

Failures are divided into two classes—those who **thought** and **never did**, and those who **did** and **never thought**.

JOHN CHARLES SALAK

People who want to be everywhere at once get nowhere.

CARL SANDBURG

Too many people miss the silver lining because they are only expecting gold.

MAURICE SETTER

If you have the will to win, you have achieved half your success; if you don't, you have achieved half your failure.

DAVID AMBROSE

Happiness is a **butterfly** which, when pursued, is always beyond our grasp; but, if you will sit down quietly, may **alight** upon you.

NATHANIEL HAWTHORNE

I make the most
of all that comes and the
least of all that goes.

SARA TEASDALE

You cannot expect to
win unless you know why
it is that you lose.

BENJAMIN LIPSON

Everything comes
to him who hustles
while he waits.

THOMAS EDISON

If your head gets too big,
it will break your neck.

ELVIS PRESLEY

Trust your instinct to
the end, though you can
render no reason.

RALPH WALDO EMERSON

All change is not
growth, as all movement
is not forward.

ELLEN GLASGOW

He turns not back
who is bound to a star.

LEONARDO DA VINCI

Behold the turtle.
He makes progress only when
he sticks his neck out.

JAMES BRYANT CONANT

You have only this moment—**sparkling** like a **star** in your hands and **melting** like a **snowflake**. Use it before it is too late.

MARIE BEYNON RAY

Always ask God's
blessing on your work,
but don't ask Him to
do it for you.

DAME FLORA ROBSON

The man who removes a mountain begins by carrying away small stones.

CHINESE PROVERB

Well done is better than well said.

BENJAMIN FRANKLIN

Pray, for God shapes the world through prayer. Prayers are **deathless**. They outlive the lives of those who utter them.

E. M. BOUNDS

Success usually comes to those who are too busy to be looking for it.

HENRY DAVID THOREAU

Everyone who got where he is had to begin where he was.

ROBERT LOUIS STEVENSON

Failure is usually the line of least persistence.

WILFRED BEAVER

It takes twenty years to make an overnight success.

EDDIE CANTOR

A pint can't hold
a quart. If it holds a
quart than it is doing all
that can possibly be
expected of it.

MARGARET DELAND

Whenever you fall,
pick something up.

OSWALD AVERY

Knowledge is power,
but enthusiasm pulls
the switch!

IVERN BALL

It is a common **observation** that those who dwell continually upon their **expectations** are apt to become oblivious to the **requirements** of their actual situation.

CHARLES SANDERS PEIRCE

The world stands
aside to let anyone pass
who knows where
he is going.

DAVID STARR JORDAN

A good scare is worth more than good advice.

The true measure of a life is not its duration, but its donation.

Yesterday is a canceled check; **tomorrow** is a promissory note; **today** is the only cash you have—so spend it wisely.

KAY LYONS

Never let statistics be
a substitute for judgment.

HENRY CLAY

To be rich is not the
end, but only a change,
of worries.

EPICURUS

Genius is eternal patience.

MICHELANGELO

Example is not the main thing in influencing others. It is the only thing.

ALBERT SCHWEITZER

God hasn't called
me to be successful,
but He has called me
to be faithful.

MOTHER TERESA

The greatest mistake you can make is to be continually fearing you will make one.

ELBERT HUBBARD

Success and failure are equally disastrous.

TENNESSEE WILLIAMS

My mother said to me, "If you become a **soldier**, you'll end up a general; if you become a **monk**, you'll end up as the pope." Instead, I became a **painter** and wound up as Picasso.

PABLO PICASSO

We can either make ourselves miserable or we can make ourselves strong. The amount of work is the same.

CARLOS CASTANEDA

Worry doesn't help tomorrow's troubles; it just ruins today's happiness.

SOURCE UNKNOWN

Man has two ends—one to **sit** on and one to **think** with. His success or failure is always dependent on the one he uses most.

GEORGE R. KIRKPATRICK

If you want a thing done,
go; if not, send.

BENJAMIN FRANKLIN

Beware of vows made
in storms. They are often
forgotten in calms.

ENGLISH PROVERB

Pay attention to your enemies,
for they are the first to
discover your mistakes.

ANTISTHENES

The true worth of a
man is to be measured by
the objects he pursues.

MARCUS AURELIUS

The percentage
of mistakes in quick decisions
is no greater than in long,
drawn-out vacillations—
and the effect of decisiveness
itself makes things go and
creates confidence.

ANNE O'HARE McCORMICK

Defensive strategies
never have produced
ultimate victories.

GENERAL DOUGLAS MACARTHUR

To know what is right
and not do it is the worst
cowardice of all.

CONFUCIUS

Have no fear of **change** as such, and, on the other hand, no liking for it merely for its own sake.

ROBERT MOSES

The great thing
in this world is not
so much where we are,
but in what direction
we are moving.

OLIVER WENDELL HOLMES

Success has made
failures of many men.

CINDY ADAMS

Depend on the
rabbit's foot if you want,
but it sure didn't work
for the rabbit!

SOURCE UNKNOWN

44

I have been **driven** many times to **pray** on my knees, for I had the overwhelming **conviction** that there was nowhere else to go. My own wisdom and that of all about me seemed **insufficient** for the day.

ABRAHAM LINCOLN

When everything has to be right, something isn't.

STANISLAW LEC

If you desire many things, many things will seem but a few.

BENJAMIN FRANKLIN

It is not always easy to
find happiness in ourselves,
but it is downright impossible
to find it elsewhere.

SOURCE UNKNOWN

Few things can help
a person more than
to place responsibility
upon him and let him
know that you
trust him.

BOOKER T. WASHINGTON

The crisis you have to worry about most of all is the one you don't see coming.

MIKE MANSFIELD

As I grow older, I pay less attention to what people say. I just watch what they do.

ANDREW CARNEGIE

Leaders are **visionaries** with a poorly developed sense of **fear** and no concept of the odds against them. **Leaders** make the **impossible** happen.

DR. ROBERT JARVICK

Half an hour's listening is essential except when you are very busy. Then a full hour is needed.

ST. FRANCIS DE SALES

I remember the story of the old man who said on his deathbed that he had a lot of trouble in his life, most of which never happened.

The most **important thing** I have learned over the years is the difference between taking one's **work** seriously and taking one's **self** seriously. The first is **imperative**, but the second is **disastrous**.

MARGARET FONTEY

When I talked, no one listened to me. As soon as I acted, I became persuasive.

GIOUSE BORSI

Do not wish to be anything but what you are, and try to be that perfectly.

ST. FRANCIS DE SALES

It is a common experience that a problem difficult at night is resolved in the morning after the committee of sleep has worked on it.

JOHN STEINBECK

I can complain because rose bushes have thorns or rejoice because thorn bushes have roses. It's all how you look at it.

J. KENFIELD MORLEY

Never mistake motion for action.

ERNEST HEMINGWAY

At times the best way to convince someone he is wrong is to let him have his way on something.

RED O'DONNELL

If you see **ten** troubles coming down the road, you can be sure that **nine** of them will run into the ditch before they reach you.

CALVIN COOLIDGE

The most significant change in a person's life is a change of attitude. Right attitudes produce right actions.

WILLIAM J. JOHNSTON

True happiness is not attained through self-gratification, but through fidelity to a worthy purpose.

HELEN KELLER

An act of **love** that fails is just as much a part of the **divine** as an act of love that succeeds; for love is measured by its own **fullness**, not by its **reception**.

HAROLD LOUKES

Persistent people
begin their success where
others end in failure.

EDWARD EGGLESTON

Be wary of any
person who urges an
action in which he himself
incurs no risk.

JOAQUIN SETANI

You must always have long-range goals to keep you from getting frustrated by short-range failures.

CHARLES C. NOBLE

All the beautiful
sentiments in the world
weigh less than a single
lovely action.

JAMES RUSSELL LOWELL

Your future depends
on many things, but
mostly on you.

FRANK TYGER

The ability to simplify
means to eliminate the
unnecessary so that the
necessary may speak.

HANS HOFMANN

Aerodynamically, the **bumble-bee** shouldn't be able to **fly**; but the bumblebee doesn't know this, so it goes on flying **anyway**.

MARY KAY ASH

Our decisions in life are often right, but the reasons for those decisions are often wrong.

Energy and persistence can conquer all things.

BENJAMIN FRANKLIN

Where there is no vision, people perish.

RALPH WALDO EMERSON

Make no little plans. They have no magic to stir men's blood.

DANIEL BURNHAM

God is our refuge and **strength**, a very present **help** in times of trouble. Therefore we will not **fear**, though the earth should **change**, though the mountains **shake** in the heart of the sea.

THE BIBLE, PSALM 46:1-2.

If you board a train going the wrong way, it is no use running along the corridor in the other direction.

DIETRICH BONHOEFFER

What we love we shall grow to resemble.

BERNARD OF CLAIRVAUX

Thinking without constructive action becomes a disease.

HENRY FORD

People will forget how fast you did a job, but they will remember how well you did it.

HOWARD W. NEWTON

You must be holy in the way God asks you to be holy. God does not ask you to be a Trappist monk or a hermit. He wills that you sanctify your everyday life.

SAINT VINCENT PALLOTTI

True success is overcoming the fear of being unsuccessful.

PAUL SWEENEY

The best bet is to bet on yourself.

ARNOLD H. GLASOW

In order to be utterly **happy** the only necessary thing is to refrain from **comparing** this moment with other moments in the **past**, which I often did not enjoy because I was **comparing** them with other moments in the **future**.

ANDRÉ GIDE

To live only for some future goal is shallow. It's the sides of the mountain that sustain life, not the top.

ROBERT M. PIRSIG

Always aim for achievement and forget about success.

HELEN HAYES

Adversity reveals genius, prosperity conceals it.

HORACE

My father used to **play** with my brother and me in the yard. Mother would come out and say, "You're **tearing up** the grass." My dad would reply, "We're not raising **grass**; we're raising **boys**."

HARMON KILLEBREW

By a small sample you may judge the whole piece.

MIGUEL DE CERVANTES

Success is going from failure to failure without losing your enthusiasm.

ABRAHAM LINCOLN

Our doubts are traitors, and make us lose the good we often might win, by fearing to attempt.

WILLIAM SHAKESPEARE

People seldom improve
when they have no other model
but themselves to copy.

OLIVER GOLDSMITH

**When nobody around
you seems to measure up,
it's time for you to check
your yardstick.**

BILL LEMLEY

Don't bother just to be better than your contemporaries or predecessors. Try to be better than yourself.

WILLIAM FAULKNER

Worry is interest paid on trouble before it comes due.

WILLIAM RALPH INGE

Half of the **unhappiness** in this world is due to the **failure** of plans which were never **reasonable** in the first place, and often **impossible**.

EDGAR WATSON HOWE

If you want to hit
the mark, you must aim
a little above it; every
arrow that flies feels the
attraction of earth.

HENRY WADSWORTH LONGFELLOW

For everyone
who makes himself
great will be humbled,
and everyone who
humbles himself will
be made great.

THE BIBLE, LUKE 14:11

A **gossip** is one who talks to you about **others**; a **bore** is one who talks to you about **himself**; a brilliant **conversationalist** is one who talks to you about **yourself**.

LISA KIRK

It isn't that people can't
see the solution, it's that they
can't see the problem.

G. K. CHESTERTON

It is not well for a
person to pray cream
and live skim milk.

HENRY WARD BEECHER

No great thing is created suddenly, any more than a bunch of grapes or even a fig. If you tell me that you desire a fig, I answer you that there must be time. It first must blossom, then bear fruit, and then ripen.

EPICTETUS

Wisdom is made up of ten parts, nine of which are silence—and the tenth is brevity.

There is not enough darkness in all the world to put out the light of even the smallest candle.

ROBERT ALDEN

When all else is lost, the future still remains.

CHRISTIAN BOVEE

When one door of **happiness** closes, another surely opens; but often we look so long at the **closed** door that we do not see the one which has been **opened** for us.

HELEN KELLER

Fear not that thy life
shall come to an end, but
rather that it shall never
have a beginning.

JOHN HENRY CARDINAL NEWMAN

The less you talk, the
more you're listened to.

ABIGAIL VAN BUREN

The art of dealing with people is the foremost secret of successful individuals. One's success in handling people is the very yardstick by which the outcome of his whole life is measured.

PAUL C. PACKE

The harder the **conflict**, the more glorious the **triumph**. What we obtain too **cheaply**, we esteem to **lightly**; 'tis **dearness** only that gives everything its **value**.

THOMAS PAINE

A thankful heart is not only the greatest virtue, but the parent of all other virtues.

CICERO

When a man is wrapped up in himself, he makes a very small package indeed.

JOHN RUSKIN

94

The very first condition
of lasting happiness is
that a life should be full
of purpose, aiming at
something outside self.

HUGH BLACK

There are two
days of the week about
which I never worry:
One of these is yester-
day and the other
day is tomorrow.

ROBERT JONES BURDETTE

You might as well fall
flat on your face as lean
over too far backward.

JAMES THURBER

Things may come to those
who wait, but only the things left
by those who hustle.

ABRAHAM LINCOLN

The **rung** of a ladder was never meant to **rest** upon, but only to hold a person's foot long enough to **enable** him to put the other somewhat **higher**.

THOMAS H. HUXLEY

None are so old as
those who have outlived
enthusiasm.

HENRY DAVID THOREAU

God does not ask your
ability or your inability. He asks
only your availability.

MARY KAY ASH

It is better to be boldly decisive and risk being wrong than to agonize at length and be right too late.

MARILYN MOATS KENNEDY

Compare what you **want** with what you **have**, and you'll be unhappy; compare what you **have** with what you **deserve**, and you'll be happy.

EVAN ESAR

Success consists of getting up just one more time than you fall.

OLIVER GOLDSMITH

The difference between getting somewhere and getting nowhere is the courage to make an early start.

CHARLES M. SCHWAB

If you can't be thankful for what you have, be thankful for what you escape.

SOURCE UNKNOWN

A life is not important except in the impact it has on other lives.

JACKIE ROBINSON

Perseverance is a
great element of success.
If you only knock long
enough and loud enough at
the gate, you are sure to
wake up somebody.

HENRY WADSWORTH LONGFELLOW

If I try to be like him, who will be like me?

YIDDISH PROVERB

The key to everything is patience. You get the chicken by hatching the egg, not by smashing it.

ARNOLD H. GLASOW

The **unthankful** heart discovers no **mercies**; but the **thankful** heart will find, in every hour, some heavenly **blessings**.

HENRY WARD BEECHER

Get a good idea, and stay with it. Dog it, and work at it until it's done, and done right.

WALT DISNEY

There are no secrets to success. It is the result of preparation, hard work, and learning from failure.

GENERAL COLIN POWELL

We act as though **comfort** and **luxury** were the chief requirements of life, when all that we need to make us really **happy** is something to be **enthusiastic** about.

CHARLES KINGSLEY

He who reflects too
much will achieve little.

J.C.F. VON SCHILLER

The truth of a thing
is the feel of it,
not the think of it.

STANLEY KUBRICK

We may our ends by our beginnings know.

SIR JOHN DENHAM

No one would have crossed the ocean if he could have gotten off the ship in the storm.

CHARLES F. KETTERING

Help others get ahead. You will always stand taller with someone else on your shoulders.

BOB MOAWAD

Human happiness and moral duty are inseparably connected.

GEORGE WASHINGTON

There is a time for departure even when there is no certain place to go.

TENNESSEE WILLIAMS

As long as you keep a person down, some part of you has to be down there to **hold** him **down**. This means that you cannot **soar** as **high** as you otherwise might.

MARIAN ANDERSON

The main dangers in
this life are the people who
want to change everything...
or nothing.

LADY ASTOR

Success is blocked
by concentrating on it
and planning for it.
Success is shy—it
won't come out while
you're watching.

TENNESSEE WILLIAMS

Whenever I remember that long-ago first day of school, only one memory shines through: **my father held my hand**.

MARCELENE COX

In case of doubt,
always decide in favor
of what is correct.

KARL KRAUS

If your ship doesn't come in, swim out to it.

JONATHAN WINTERS

118

About the Authors

Bret Nicholaus and Paul Lowrie are the authors of 17 books, including the national bestsellers *The Conversation Piece* and *The Christmas Conversation Piece*; other popular titles include *KidChat*, *The Christmas Letters*, *Lemonade Lessons for Life*, and *Who We Are*. The goal of all their books is to provide the reader with content that is highly positive and uplifting. Nicholaus and his family live in the Chicago area; Lowrie lives in South Dakota. If you would like to learn more about the authors or their books, you can do so by connecting to their website, www.williamrandallpublishing.com.

JUDE 24-25

William Randall Publishing

publishes books that inspire people
of all ages to imagine the impossible,
to discover the profound in the ordinary,
and to keep life always in its proper perspective.

Our books are available in bookstores
everywhere. For a free catalog of our
complete line of fine books, contact:

William Randall Publishing
P.O. Box 340
Yankton, SD 57078

Phone: (605) 660-0335
Fax: (605) 260-6873

Email: questmarc@mail.com
Website: www.williamrandallpublishing.com